MW00578479

MADE FOR GREATNESS

A GROWTH MINDSET JOURNAL FOR COURAGEOUS CATHOLIC YOUTH

GINNY KOCHIS

For my children. May you always have a heart for God.

CONTENTS

Want to hear something amazing?

Our universe is host to approximately one billion, trillion stars. That's not a small number, and still, *new* stars are discovered all the time.

It's also pretty amazing when you consider the number of animals - do you know how many exist? There's no exact count, but scientists estimate there are between five and 30 million different species. 300,000 of those species are *just beetles alone.*

And what about people? In 2019, the US Census Bureau estimated over 7.7 billion people live on the Earth's surface. 360,000 babies are born *each day.*

- One billion, trillion stars.
- Five to 30 million animal species.
- 7.7 billion (and counting!) people

Plus you.

Kinda makes you wonder, doesn't it? Why did God create you, too?

Why You?

If we look at the world based on numbers alone, it's clear God excels at creation. There are so many beautiful people and animals and places, it's hard to imagine how one individual would matter at all!

But you do matter. Because after God looked at those beautiful people and animals and places, he decided the world still needed you:

the only person designed to look like you, talk like you, be like you;

the only human being created to do exactly what God has determined;

And *that,* my friend, is pretty cool.

Sometimes, though, life isn't easy. You run into challenges and road-blocks. No matter how hard you work or try to find the answer, you get stuck, fall behind, or fail.

You start to think, "Forget it. I'm done with this business." You'd rather give up and move on to something else.

I get it. It feels more comfortable to quit. But as Pope Emeritus Benedict XVI has said, you were not made for comfort. You were made for greatness.

This book will help you learn that about yourself.

A Life of Growth and Virtue

God has started a good work within you, and He will be faithful to complete it (see Philippians 1:6).

But when life's struggles drag you down, you can develop what's called a fixed mindset: a consistent feeling of "stuck-ness" you can't seem to improve.

You say things like:

"I think I'll sit out for this soccer game. I'm not good, anyway."

"This math lesson is impossible. I'm not even going to use it later in life."

"I've never been good at drawing. That's totally my sister's thing."

You may not be called to a career as a professional athlete, a mathematician, or a graphic designer. You might not be called to give grand concerts or perform as a principal dancer on stage. But you are called to something: a life of growth and virtue. God

uses your struggles to mold you into the person He wants you to become.

What is Virtue?

A virtue is a firm, consistent desire to do what is good. The virtues help you give your best in every endeavor and work for the good of those around you. They help you choose to do what is good and right through your actions, thoughts, and words.

What is a Growth Mindset?

A growth mindset is a constant decision to see challenge as an opportunity for growth. It helps you achieve your goals as you embrace perseverance and hard work. You develop a growth mindset naturally as you live out the virtues.

There are a total of seven virtues. The first four are called the Cardinal virtues; the remaining three are called Theological:

- Prudence: also called wisdom, prudence helps differentiate between what is right and what is wrong
- Temperance: encourages moderation. It helps you develop self-control
- Justice: when you seek what is right and good for all people
- Fortitude: the courage to do what is right
- Faith: allows you to believe in all of God's promises
- Hope: the ability to trust in God
- Charity: the ability to love God first, and through that love, serve your neighbors

God never promised your time on Earth would be easy, but that struggle is what refines you in the end. This is how a true growth mindset rooted in Catholic teaching differs from the version the world offers. Contrary to what popular belief may tell you, you are made for the heart of God.

How to use this book

This workbook is divided into seven chapters, one for each of the virtues.

- You'll find inspirational stories of saints and holy men and women who endured great difficulty to live their lives for God
- You'll encounter passages from Scripture and quotes from the saints paired with questions to help you apply them to your life
- You'll read stories from contemporary young people who have overcome great obstacles and seen God's promises on the other side
- You'll learn to apply the virtues to your own life and make a step-by-step plan to grow in virtue and growth mindset

You can work through this journal with a parent, friend, or teacher. You can work through it on your own. You can do it all at once or take a week, a month, or even a season for each virtue.

Go at a pace that's comfortable and ask God for his guidance and grace.

1
———

THE FIRST VIRTUE: PRUDENCE

GROWTH MINDSET PRINCIPLE: CHOOSING TO DO WHAT IS
RIGHT

As a Cardinal virtue, prudence helps you determine the difference between what is right and what is wrong. From a growth mindset perspective, prudence helps you make the right choices, such as when to ask for help, when to rethink what you're doing, and how to know which obstacles are the right ones to attack.

THINK of someone you know who has made good, holy decisions, even when that decision was hard to make. Who is it? What choice was this person facing? What impression did that leave on you?

Prudence in Action

St. Therese of Lisieux
>   Born: January 2, 1878
>   Died: September 30, 1897

It's hard to imagine the saints as little kids. But St. Therese of Lisieux (the Little Flower) was a child once, and boy, was she wild.

Therese was the baby of the family. She had a temper, was rather selfish, and was often described as difficult. But on Christmas Eve of 1886, Therese had a drastic change of heart. She devoted her life to Jesus and let go of her own desires. A few years later, she entered the Carmelite convent and became a bride of Christ.

Despite Therese's devotion to the Father, her journey to sainthood was far from a breeze. She still had to work to embrace the virtue of prudence, especially with her Sisters in Christ.

Therese struggled to have patience with irritating people, specifically one of her fellow nuns. Therese could barely stand to be in the same room as this sister. In fact, Therese wrote that the nun's presence made her want to run in the opposite direction - fast!

Therese knew it would be wrong to treat her poorly, even though to be kind was very hard. Therese offered her negative feelings to God instead of showing any sign of frustration:

Each time she encountered her fellow nun in the convent, Therese would compliment the sister and say a prayer of Thanksgiving for her life. Not only that, Therese went out of her way to do thoughtful acts for the sister despite her irritation. Eventually, the negative feelings disappeared and were replaced with sweetness.

Therese made a clear decision to treat her kindly, even when it was overwhelmingly hard.

Stop and Think

St. Therese did everything in her power to avoid revealing her irritation with her fellow sister. What might have been the easier way out? Which path would you have taken, and why?

Just For Fun

What's your favorite thing to do when you need a break? How does it help you recharge?

Making the Right Decision

When you're faced with a difficult decision, it's hard to know which choice is the
proper path. You can use a process called
discernment to help you prayerfully determine what God wants.

Think about a tough decision you're
facing. What are your choices? List them
here:

ONCE YOU'VE WRITTEN down your options, find a quiet space. Ask the
Holy Spirit to guide you as you think about the following questions.

- Which choice will help me grow in holiness?
- Which choice is like other good choices I've made before?
- Which choice makes me feel peaceful and at rest?
- What about people who care about my salvation (like my
  parents or my pastor)? What do they say about my
  choices?
- Which choice is on my heart after prayer?

GOD WOULD NEVER
INSPIRE ME WITH
DESIRES WHICH
CANNOT BE
REALIZED; SO IN
SPITE OF MY
LITTLENESS, I CAN
HOPE TO BE A

SAINT

-St. Therese of Lisieux

STOP AND THINK

HOW DOES the story of St. Therese change the way you look at decisions you have made? What would you do differently, and why?

Let Us Pray

Heavenly Father, be with me. Send your Holy Spirit so that I will always know what is good and pleasing to you. Guide me, Lord, to be prudent in all my thoughts, words, and actions. Help me to live out the virtue of prudence so that I can do all things with your help.

AMEN.

Hearing God's Voice

1 Thessalonians 5:12-22

REJOICE ALWAYS, pray without ceasing, give thanks in all circumstances; for this is the will of God in Christ Jesus for you. Do not quench the Spirit. Do not despise the words of prophets, but test everything; hold fast to what is good; abstain from every form of evil.

WHAT DO you think it means to "test everything"?

HOW DO *you* test everything when it's time to make a decision?

Prudence in Action - Melanie's Story

When Melanie Philomena D'Souza was 17 years old, she left her native country, Oman, and moved to the U.S. to live, study, and work. She was nervous about leaving her Catholic community in Oman, but Melanie felt right at home in the American Catholic Church.

For six years, Melanie studied architecture and worked all over the U.S. But one day, Melanie received notice that her work visa would not be renewed (a visa is a document that allows citizens from other countries to live and work in the United States). Melanie had to go back to Oman.

The transition home would not be easy. Shortly before Melanie received news about her visa, Oman's government ruled only those educated in that country could work as architects. Not only would Melanie miss her friends and American Catholic community, but she also wouldn't be able to find a job.

Melanie knew that to stay in the U.S. illegally would be dishonest. Determined to do the right thing, Melanie turned her sadness into something positive. She asked her home pastor's permission to start the Don Bosco Book Club for Catholic young adults. In six months, the group grew from five to 14 members: amazing growth for a Catholic community in a Muslim country. Book club members read the works of the saints and Church leaders together, discussing them and growing in friendship and faith.

Of her story, Melanie says, "Where [God] closes the door, he opens the window. I have learned that when I attach myself to the world too much, He helps me recognize it, humbles me, and shows me even more of the world, including alternative routes."

Time to Reflect

Look back at the beginning of this chapter. Before you began reading, how did you feel about making hard decisions? How do you feel about it now?

WHAT STORY, scripture, quotation, or question stood out to you the most over the course of the chapter? Why? How will it make a difference in your life?

Step by Step

Let's craft a plan for the next time you face hard decisions. Choose from the discernment options on the next page. In the space provided:

1. list the steps you'd like to take to help you make the right decision
2. add any additional ideas you might have.

When the time comes to make a decision, refer back to your plan.

- Talk to your parents
- Pray about your decision
- Read passages from the Psalms or Proverbs for inspiration
- Pay attention and stay focused during Mass
- Receive the Sacraments
- Make a pro/con list about your decision
- Talk to faithful friends
- Talk to your pastor
- Look/listen for a feeling of peace

THE SECOND VIRTUE: TEMPERANCE

GROWTH MINDSET PRINCIPLE: RESOLVING TO STAY ON TASK

E ver get stuck in a video game binge session or eat too much of your sister's birthday cake? You probably could have used a little bit of temperance - the ability to take a step back and "say when."

Temperance is self-control. It's the virtue that helps you moderate your physical desires and prevents you from going overboard. When you're working on a growth mindset, it's the virtue that keeps you focused. Temperance makes aware of and involved in the task at hand.

Think of someone you know who has great self-control. Who is it? What example has this person set for you?

Temperance in Action:

Venerable Teresita Quevedo
    Born: April 12, 1930
    Died: April 8, 1950

VENERABLE TERESITA QUEVEDO WAS PRETTY. She was popular. And she had a well-intentioned mischievous side that drove her parents and teachers nuts.

But Teresita had another side. Amid the dances, games, and parties she attended, Teresita felt a call she couldn't ignore. Yes, Teresita loved driving up and down the basketball court with determination, and yes, she loved driving her dad's car rather fast. But Teresita loved Our Lord and the Blessed Virgin more deeply and with a great desire for holiness.

By the time she was 17 and one of the most popular girls at her high school, Teresita had entered the convent and left the secular world behind.

Teresita knew a great deal about herself and her personality. In order to devote herself fully to Christ in her vocation, she would have to cast aside her distractions. The virtue of temperance shifted her joy and zeal for the fast lane to her vocation, allowing her to apply it to the religious life.

Teresita's life proves that to be holy, you don't have to stop being yourself. Also, Teresita's choices show you the value of temperance, that it's helpful to keep your blinders on. The shiny temptations of life can distract you from your goals and heavenly aspirations. Thanks to Venerable Teresita Quevedo, you can see the value of self-control.

Stop and Think:

When Teresita discerned her call to the religious life, the virtue of temperance helped her let go of earthly pleasures. How did surrendering these things help Teresita pursue her vocation?

Just for Fun:

What would you do if you woke up one morning to discover the whole world was made of candy?

∽

The Ants and the Grasshopper: Aesop's Temperance Tale

Do you know Aesop's tale of the ants and the grasshopper?

In it, a grasshopper meets a group of ants storing grain for the winter. He invites the ants to play music and dance with him in the summer sunlight. Busy and industrious, the ants say no.

The grasshopper thinks the ants are silly; why gather food when it is summer and there's so much fun to be had? A few months later, the grasshopper is hungry, cold, and miserable.

The ants, on the other hand, have plenty of built-up stores.

It's easy to identify with the grasshopper, isn't it? Making music, dancing, and having fun doing so are great. But what happens when a pastime is so shiny, so attractive and tempting, that it throws you off course?

You're left empty-handed, disappointed, and full of regret and sorrow. It's not a fun place to be at all.

Distractions are all around you. They are fully capable of dragging you aside. Sometimes, it's glaringly obvious: who wouldn't prefer to go swimming instead of mowing the lawn or taking the trash out? Most of the time, though, it's less noticeable:

"I'll just do five more minutes on this video game..."

"Just three more baskets - for practice..."

Five minutes stretches into 30; three baskets become a game of four on four.

As you work to develop your growth mindset, embrace temperance and self control. You'll be able to put off for the moment something fun and exciting for something beautiful down the road.

MOTHER,

GRANT THAT
EVERYONE WHO
LOOKS AT ME MAY
SEE

YOU.

-Venerable Teresita
Quevedo

Stop and Think

Distractions aren't always shiny: they can be negative attitudes and self-talk. What are your distractions, both negative and positive? How would your life be different if you cut those distractions out?

Let Us Pray

Lord, you granted Venerable Teresita Quevedo the virtue of temperance. Through your grace, Teresita was able to surrender to your will and devote herself to you. Grant that I may also develop the virtue of temperance so that I might let go of distractions and pursue your holy will for my life.

Amen

Hearing God's Voice

"All things are lawful for me," but not all things are beneficial. "All things are lawful for me," but I will not be dominated by anything." 1 Cor 6:12

What things in your life are not helping you? In other words, what might be dominating (or controlling) you, preventing you from completing your tasks?

Temperance in Action: Your Story

 In the last chapter, you read the story of Melanie D'Souza and her prudent decision to stay the course. This is a space for you to write about your own journey with temperance. How have you used the virtue of temperance to stay focused and on task? If you haven't yet, how could you do so in the future?

∾

Time to Reflect

What does temperance mean to you now that you've read the chapter?

WHAT STORY, scripture, quotation, or question stood out to you the most over the course of the chapter? Why? What's your greatest take-away - the nugget of information you will carry with you?

Step by Step

Remember the distractions you identified earlier? List them again, this time in order of least distracting to most.

How can you fight these distractions?

What reminders can you create for yourself when temptation starts to drag you aside?

Choose a motto - a personal statement that will support you when you're chasing a shiny object. Look up scripture passages on diligence and encouraging quotes from favorite saints for ideas.

3

THE THIRD VIRTUE: FORTITUDE

GROWTH MINDSET PRINCIPLE: COURAGE IN THE FACE OF
DIFFICULTY

T he third Cardinal virtue, fortitude is the ability to do what is good and right all the time, even when doing so might be very hard. Fortitude gives you the courage to pick yourself up and keep going after you stumble and fall.

Do you know of anyone (in real life, history, or fiction) who has shown great courage? What challenges did this person face? How did he or she act courageously?

Fortitude in Action:

Venerable Augustus Tolton
  Born: April 1, 1854
  Died: July 9, 1897

IT WAS dark on the bank of the Mississippi River the night Augustus Tolton clung to the folds of his mother's skirt. They were runaway slaves on the edge of freedom, fleeing into Illinois.

Some white northerners viewed freed slaves with distrust. Augustus and his siblings were denied entry into the local school building. His family also wished to go to Mass and receive the Sacraments, but most of the Churches were hesitant to let them come - until the Toltons met Fr. Peter McGirr.

An Irish pastor in Quincy, Illinois, Fr. McGirr welcomed the Tolton family. He was impressed by Augustus' piety and desire to learn. The Tolton children began school at McGirr's parish; a few months later, McGirr began preparing Augustus for the seminary.

Augustus studied for the priesthood in Rome because American seminaries denied him admission. He excelled in his studies and became the first African-American ordained to the priesthood on April 24, 1886.

Even after his ordination, Fr. Tolton faced criticism and distrust. Still, he founded one African-American mission and two African-American parishes. Each community flourished: one grew from 30 parishioners to 600 in just a few months.

Fr. Tolton evangelized in the streets of Chicago day and night, year-round. Known as "Good Fr. Gus," many Church historians credit Fr. Tolton's service as the driving force behind the growth of the African-American Catholic community after the Civil War.

Stop and Think

How did Fr. Tolton show courage? What makes his actions a good example of the virtue of fortitude?

Just for Fun

If you could build the best fort ever, what would it include? Where would you build it? How would you make it? Draw and write about it below.

Building a Fortress Brain

Your brain is a complex organ, capable of processing 100 trillion instructions in a single second. It has 250,000,000 GB of storage space and creates enough electricity to power a 25-watt bulb.

Your brain is beautiful, amazing, and powerful. It is also capable of derailing you from your goals.

Think about the challenges you may have faced recently:

- School subjects that require extra effort.
- Team tryouts or auditions that don't turn out as you'd hoped.
- Hobbies or skills you've tried to learn that have taken more time - and practice than you expected.

Your brain's reaction to these challenges will either propel you forward or prevent you from charging on.

Your brain likes to form predictable responses it can rely on all the time. Take pickles, for example - especially if you don't like them. Your brain is trained to say "no, thank you." It's hard to convince yourself to give them another try.

The same goes for those challenges (and others) we were talking about earlier. Instead of a fixed mindset about pickles, you have a fixed mindset about life. You have to train your brain for fortitude by creating new pathways.

How do you do that?

When you ask for help to understand a math problem

When you practice soccer drills against an old brick wall

When you pick yourself up, dust yourself off, and return to your desk, the field, or the stage with courage, that frees your brain from the tyranny of "I can't do this" and replaces it with "I'll keep trying."

You build positive habits that, while they won't always be easy, will help you become the person God desires.

THE CATHOLIC CHURCH DEPLORES A DOUBLE SLAVERY - THAT OF THE MIND AND THAT OF THE BODY. SHE ENDEAVORS TO FREE US OF BOTH.

-Venerable Augustus Tolton

Stop and Think

In this quote, Fr. Tolton talks about two kinds of slavery: one of the body (like that of African slaves) and one of the mind (for example, a fixed mindset). How can the virtue of fortitude work against slavery of the mind?

Let Us Pray

Heavenly Father, your servant Augustus Tolton pursued his vocation with great fortitude and courage. Help me to develop the same courage Fr. Tolton showed as I follow the path you have set for me. Grant me the courage to become the person you desire.

AMEN

Hearing God's Voice

"My brothers and sisters, whenever you face trials of any kind, consider it nothing but joy, because you know that the testing of your faith produces endurance." James 1:2-3

HOW WOULD you write this in your own words? Rephrase what James has written and share your response with your parents.

HOW OFTEN HAVE you been joyful in the face of trials? Was it easy? Or did you find it hard? Why?

Fortitude in Action: Fouad's Story

During his second year of college, photographer and writer Fouad Abou-Rizk went skiing with his PE class. While there, Fouad collided face-first at high speed with a metal railing. The impact broke his jaw and to heal it, doctors had to wire it shut.

Fouad had been keeping a journal to record his daily prayers in the months leading up to his accident. Each message to God began with a statement of praise and gratitude: "God, thank you for another good day on planet Earth."

The night after Fouad broke his jaw, he wrote the same statement, but crossed out the word "good." It was a huge challenge to thank God for his life, but he did it anyway. "I knew that no matter how bad the pain was, every day was a [gift] because God loves me and cares for me." Fouad's courage and fortitude kept him from giving up.

Several years after his accident, Fouad looks at his experience as an opportunity for growth. He often reflects on Philippians 4:7:

"Then the peace of God that surpasses all understanding will guard your hearts and minds in Christ Jesus."

That verse helps Fouad to endure suffering in peace knowing God's love will not abandon him. Fouad encourages anyone facing an obstacle to remember each day is a good day, even when it seems horrible.

"God [loves] you," he says, and that is "the reason to endure."

Time to Reflect

How has this chapter changed how you feel about persevering through difficulty?

WHAT STORY, scripture, quotation, or question stood out to you the most? Why? What's your greatest takeaway - the nugget of information you will carry with you?

STEP BY STEP

We've already talked a little about changing your brain's habits. Now it's time to face your struggles head-on.

FIRST, think about the challenges and obstacles you have overcome. List them below.

1. FOR EACH challenge you conquered, think back to *how* you overcame that difficulty.

. . .

2. WHAT STEPS did you take to overcome it? What did you learn from the challenge? List the steps and lessons below.

3. WHAT OBSTACLES and challenges are you facing now? What are some challenges that have been difficult for you to overcome? List them here.

4. LOOK BACK at number two. How can you use your answers there to help you get through the obstacles in number three?

THE FOURTH VIRTUE: JUSTICE

GROWTH MINDSET PRINCIPLE: GIVING OUR BEST TO THOSE
WHO DEPEND ON US

The final Cardinal virtue, justice is the obligation to seek what is good for your neighbor and act accordingly. It's a habit that helps you recognize each person's dignity. This will help you give your best to people who depend on you (like teammates) and to those whose authority you are under (like parents, teachers, spiritual directors, and God). Justice is setting your mind to do hard things for others because of the respect they deserve as a child of God.

Do you know someone who works hard to help others? Who is it? Whom does this person serve?

Justice in Action:

St. Martin de Porres
  Born: December 9, 1579
  Died: November 3, 1639

IN 1594, a 15-year-old boy named Martin volunteered as a janitor at the Dominicans of the Holy Rosary Priory in Lima, Peru. Martin's father was a Spaniard; his mother was a freed slave of native origin. His heritage prevented him from entering a religious order.

But Martin longed for the religious life, so he entered the only way he could. As a janitor, he was hard-working, kind, and overwhelmingly generous. His superior was impressed by his work ethic: he made Martin a lay member of the Dominican order when Martin turned 24.

Ten years later, Martin was assigned to the infirmary. He cared for every patient, regardless of race, color, or wealth. Martin didn't care where his patients came from; he didn't care how sick or dirty they were. He treated each person with dignity and gave every patient his due.

Martin's habit of justice extended beyond the walls of the infirmary. He founded a home for freed slaves and abandoned children. He often took the poor, the seriously ill, and the homeless into his own room at the Priory. Legend has it that Martin even cared for the animals in and around the Priory: apparently, he led an entire colony of mice to safety outside the Priory after the Prior threatened to adopt a cat.

Martin de Porres died on November 3, 1663. His dedication to serving all people regardless of need or station earned him sainthood: he was canonized by Pope John XXIII in 1962.

Stop and Think

Share the story of St. Martin de Porres with your parents or a friend. How is St. Martin's story an example of justice?

Just for Fun

If you could travel to any place in the world, where would it be, and why? Draw or write about it here.

Justice: the Community Virtue

So far, our journal focus has been on the impact of the virtues on you:

- Prudence helps you make wise decisions
- Temperance helps you develop self-control
- Fortitude offers courage when you feel like quitting or giving up the battle

Justice is a little different. This virtue has the greatest outward impact on others rather than on you.

God desires you to live in the community. Your first community is your family; as you grow, it branches farther out into the world. Like the missing piece of a jigsaw puzzle, your determination and drive matter to your community.

- Quitting the play halfway through rehearsal season is not justice. It leaves your cast members in the lurch.
- Dropping your part of a group project is not justice. Your partners need the contribution of your work.
- Saying to yourself, "I'm worthless! I'm no good at this!" is not justice. It is hurtful to God who made you (and as the old saying goes, God doesn't make junk).

It's easy to think of justice as equality, or, as the world often views it, revenge. But in reality, it's the virtue that recognizes each person's dignity and the respect he is afforded, and how you can offer that to a child of God.

EVERYTHING, EVEN
SWEEPING,
SCRAPING
VEGETABLES,
WEEDING A GARDEN
AND WAITING ON
THE SICK COULD BE
A PRAYER, IF IT
WERE OFFERED TO
GOD.

-Mary Fabyan Windeatt,
St. Martin De Porres: The
Story of the Little Doctor
of Lima, Peru

Stop and Think

Share Mary Fabyan Windeatt's quote with your parents or a friend.
Tell them what you have learned about justice. Together, determine
how his daily efforts to pray through service are an example of the
virtue of justice. To whom was St. Martin giving his due?

Let Us Pray

Heavenly Father, your servant Martin de Porres embodied the virtue of justice. Help me to be like him, to seek what is right in every situation and give my fellow humanity its due.

Amen

Hearing God's Voice

"He has told you, O mortal, what is good;

and what does the Lord require of you

but to do justice, and to love kindness,

and to walk humbly with your God?"

Micah 6:8

What is humility? What is kindness? How do justice, kindness, and humility work together to please the Lord?

Justice in Action: Your Story

How have you been a valuable part of your community? How have
you recognized another person's dignity and continued your part of
the bargain, even when the bargain was hard?

Time to Reflect

What does justice mean to you now that you've read the chapter?

WHAT STORY, scripture, quotation, or question stood out to you the most? Why? What's your greatest takeaway - the nugget of information you will carry with you?

Step by Step

From a growth mindset perspective, justice helps you to be mindful of the way your actions impact others. In the moment, however, when you are frustrated and discouraged, it can be difficult to think about anyone else.

Make a list of the people who depend on you. This can include family members, teammates, friends, teachers, or coaches.

Now that you have made your list, consider how you can treat each of those people with dignity and justice. In the space below, write down how you can give each person what he deserves as a child of God.

5

THE FIFTH VIRTUE: FAITH

GROWTH MINDSET PRINCIPLE: BELIEVING YOU ARE MADE IN
THE IMAGE AND LIKENESS OF GOD

Faith is a beautiful gift, one that allows us to believe in the Truths God has revealed to us. Without faith, you'd have a hard time believing in the mysteries of the Eucharist, the Trinity, or the Incarnation. How amazing that God gives you the means to believe in His promises!

One of God's promises can be the hardest to remember, though. It's the truth that you are made in His image and likeness; that He has designed you for a specific purpose. Faith helps you embrace that truth and move forward, confident in your efforts. God has made you unique and unrepeatable. His plan for you is holy and good.

Think of a person you know who has great trust in God. How can you tell this person is faithful?

Faith in Action:

Mother Mary Angelica of the Assumption (Mother Angelica)
　　Born: April 20, 1923
　　Died: March 27, 2016

MOTHER ANGELICA WAS BORN Rita Rizzo in a poor area of Canton, Ohio. At 16, Rita developed a painful stomach illness. She prayed a novena to St. Therese for her healing. On the third day of the novena, Rita was healed.

The miracle transformed Rita. She decided to give herself completely to God. Rita became a Poor Clare in 1945 and took the name Sister Mary Angelica of the Assumption. Over the next 50 years, Mother Angelica devoted herself to building the Eternal Word Television Network (EWTN) to reach minority populations and the poor.

Mother Angelica faced many hurdles while building EWTN. In order to reach the number of people Mother Angelica wanted, EWTN would require two satellite dishes the order couldn't afford. Mother Angelica ordered them anyway; someone donated the exact amount needed to cover it all.

Stories of such miracles abound in the founding of EWTN's ministry. The station's antenna, in fact, is high on a mountain, surrounded by thousands of trees. But the signal is strong and the antenna works perfectly. Mother Angelica says St. Michael led her there.

Mother Angelica had deep faith in the Lord and his providence for her. Through her faith, she has helped change the world.

Stop and Think

Based on what you know about faith so far, how is Mother Angelica's story an example of faith? Share what you've learned about her with your parents. Write down some of the moments in Mother Angelica's life where she exhibited great faith in God.

Just for Fun

Mother Angelica loved to tell jokes like these:

- "The apostles were dodos, dummies. But all the smart people in the world at the time wouldn't take chances. That is the same problem we have today. The world is looking for intellectuals and the Lord is looking for dummies. That's why I'm here."
- "The sisters say I have the eighth gift of the Holy Spirit: guts!"

What's your favorite joke?
Share it here:

His Eye Is on the Sparrow - and It's Definitely on You, Too.

You are made for greatness, and God wants to get you there.

It's hard to wrap your head around that, isn't it, especially when failure and setbacks come around. It's easy to feel betrayed, weighed down, and broken like you're worth nothing and nothing is worth trying.

But God has revealed the truth to you. You are made in the image and likeness of God.

God sent His son for your salvation, a savior who is fully human and divine. Jesus knows your struggles; just think of his Passion, death, and Resurrection. You are called to redemptive suffering, the act of picking up your burden with Jesus and letting it bring you closer to God.

So, my friend, take a lesson from Mother Angelica. When it seems like the world is against you, and when you feel like just giving up?

Have faith. The Lord is with you. You are worth many sparrows. Remember to put your trust in God.

SIMPLY BELIEVING
IN THE EXISTENCE
OF GOD IS NOT
EXACTLY WHAT I
WOULD CALL A
COMMITMENT.
AFTER ALL, EVEN
THE DEVIL BELIEVES
THAT GOD EXISTS.
BELIEVING HAS TO
CHANGE THE WAY
WE LIVE.
-Mother Angelica

Stop and Think

Share this quote with your parents or a friend. Explain what Mother Angelica means when she says "believing has to change the way we live," especially when it comes to his will for your life.

∾

Let Us Pray

Lord, Mother Angelica had such great faith in you. She understood the role you called her to and worked diligently to fulfill it. Increase my faith; help me to pick up my cross and follow you. Let me become the person you desire.

AMEN.

HEARING GOD'S VOICE

"ARE NOT two sparrows sold for a penny? Yet not one of them will fall to the ground apart from your Father. And even the hairs of your head are all counted. So do not be afraid; you are of more value than many sparrows."
Matthew 10:29-31

WHAT DOES it mean when Jesus says even the hairs of your head are all counted? How does God care for you?

Faith in Action: J.M. Kraemer's Story

In 2001, Master Builder J.M. Kraemer founded a ministry called The Lego Church Project. For two decades, he's been planning, building, and arranging for the display of Lego churches at parishes and public spaces throughout the greater Saginaw, MI area.

While The Lego Church Project is a creative way to spread the Truth of Catholicism, it's not an easy task. "I'm doing this mostly...freehand with no idea of how things will turn out," J.M. says. "The vision that I see may take some twists and turns," he says cheerfully, noting that many things in life (and Legos!) are out of our control. But these are the moments where we must rely on our faith in Christ Jesus: "We have been given the tools and resources..to find solutions to the problems at hand."

What are those tools and resources? The power of prayer and faith, of course. "Near the end of [one] build, I was reaching a point where some important parts [of the project] were not lining up correctly. No matter how I looked I could not see the problem. After spending time in prayer, I discovered one of the beams was not lined up properly...just enough to throw things off."

Prayer didn't fix J.M.'s problem; rather, "it gave me the wisdom to look for something I otherwise would not have noticed. In the same way," J.M. says, "having total faith in Christ is what gives us that ability to face our challenges." When you have faith that God will lead you through the struggle, "ideas will come and solutions will be found."

J.M. is no stranger to struggle. In addition to his skill as a Master Builder, J.M. lives with daily physical challenges from cerebral palsy and vision concerns. But during his times of struggle, J.M. prays for direction and wisdom. Our faith and our prayers "have the power to move mountains," J.M. reminds us, "if we allow God to move within [our hearts]."

Time to Reflect

Has your understanding of faith changed now that you have read the chapter? How?

WHAT STORY, scripture, quotation, or question stood out to you the most? Why? What's your greatest takeaway - the nugget of information you will carry with you?

STEP BY STEP

Remember how your brain is a creature of habit? You can develop positive habits of thought to help grow your faith in difficult times. Below is a list of suggested Scripture verses and prayers to repeat to yourself when you feel your hard work isn't worth it. Choose a few - or all - and commit them to memory. They will help to retrain your mind.

- "I believe! Help my unbelief!" Mark 9:24
- *Act of Faith*: O my God, I firmly believe that you are one God in three divine persons, Father, Son and Holy Spirit. I believe that your divine Son became man and died for our

sins, and that he will come to judge the living and the dead. I believe these and all the truths which the holy catholic Church teaches, because in revealing them you can neither deceive nor be deceived. Amen

- "For it was you who formed my inward parts; you knit me together in my mother's womb. I praise you, for I am fearfully and wonderfully made. Wonderful are your works; that I know very well." Psalm 139:13-14
- I can do all things through Christ who strengthens me Phillippians 4:13

Do you have another prayer or Scripture verse you'd like to include? Write it here:

6

THE SIXTH VIRTUE: HOPE

GROWTH MINDSET PRINCIPLE: TRUST IN GOD WHEN LIFE
IS HARD

The virtue of hope enables you to trust in God's providence: the truth that He will help you gain eternal life. In the same way that you hope in God for your salvation, you also hope in Him to achieve your dreams. God is so good that He has given you the tools you need to join Him in heaven, plus the tools you need to reach your goals.

Who's the most hopeful person you know? Why?

Hope in Action

St. Maximillian Kolbe
    Born: January 8, 1894
    Died: August 14, 1941

WHEN MAXIMILLIAN KOLBE was 12 years old, Our Lady paid him a visit. She offered him two crowns of thorns, one white and one red. The white crown represented purity and a priestly vocation. The red crown represented martyrdom.

Maximillian accepted them both.

35 years later, Maximillian was all grown up. He was a Franciscan friar, a journalist, and an amateur radio host. He refused to support the Nazi forces in Poland. They arrested him and took him to the concentration camp, Auschwitz, in February of 1941.

Auschwitz was a place of great pain and suffering. Fr. Kolbe's presence was a beacon of hope. He ministered to the inmates and was tortured for his efforts. But Fr. Kolbe never wavered in his peaceful disposition. He held fast to his devotion to the Blessed Virgin Mary and the promise he had made to her so long ago.

Fr. Kolbe had been at Auschwitz for six months when a prisoner escaped from the camp. The Nazi officers selected 10 men to starve to death as punishment. Fr. Kolbe stepped forward to take the place of one of those chosen; the man had cried out in terror of the fate of his wife and children.

Fr. Kolbe continued his ministry during this period. He prayed and encouraged his fellow prisoners for two weeks. By day 14, Kolbe was the last of the 10 still living. Nazi offers discovered the friar kneeling peacefully in prayer with a cheerful disposition. Nazi officers executed him on August 14, 1941.

Stop and Think

St. Maximillian Kolbe's story is difficult. Talk it over with your parents and, if you wish, do more research on the life and death of this great saint. Together with your parents, list three examples of hope in his life and martyrdom. Why is he a beacon of hope?

Just for Fun

Imagine yourself 30 years from now. What do you think the world will look like? What do you think your life will be like? Write about it, or draw a comic that shows your answers.

Do or Do Not - There is No Try

I grew up watching Star Wars with my family. My favorite character was Yoda, the little green Jedi Master who was as feisty and wise as he was cute. Yoda has a lot of great one-liners from the original trilogy, but his most well known is probably the one featured in the title to this section:

"Do or do not. There is no try."

If you haven't seen the movies, let me bring you up to speed. Luke is a young man on a quest to save the galaxy from the forces of evil. He meets Yoda, a short, 900-year-old wise man who begins to train Luke in the ancient ways of the Jedi. Yoda puts Luke through a series of difficult training exercises  so he can face Darth Vader, the bad guy. Luke is afraid he can't do it, but out of love and respect for Yoda, Luke promises he will try.

Yoda's not having any of it. He instructs Luke to strike the word "try" from his vocabulary - that he will either do the task in front of him or let Vader's evil consume the galaxy. Yoda has no patience for Luke's lack of hope in his abilities. He knows Luke has been chosen for something very special, and not only that, has been given the abilities to achieve it. Yoda won't let Luke approach the situation without determination and hope.

Star Wars is fiction. There is no galactic war. There is no force, and there is no such thing as a Jedi Master. But when it comes to facing the challenge before you, Yoda is right - there is no try.

As a virtue, hope leads you to trust in God for your salvation. It also grants you the knowledge He has given the way to eternal life. Just as you won't go it alone when it comes to your salvation, you won't go it alone when it comes to doing hard stuff, either. God gives you the tools you need to turn your stumbling blocks into stepping stones.

Confront the obstacles in your path with determination and perseverance. Remain faithful to God's good and holy call.

EVERY FALL, EVEN IF IT BE VERY GRAVE AND REPEATED, SERVES US ALWAYS AND ONLY AS A LITTLE STEP TOWARDS A HIGHER

PERFECTION.

-St. Maximillian Kolbe

Stop and Think

How do our falls bring us closer to perfection? (Hint: remember redemptive suffering? We talked about it in the last chapter.)

Let Us Pray

Lord, your servant Maximillian Kolbe never gave up hope, even when his days were at their darkest. Grant that I will always hope in you for my salvation, and for the plan you have for my life.

AMEN

Hearing God's Voice

"For surely I know the plans I have for you, says the Lord, plans for your welfare and not for harm, to give you a future with hope." Jeremiah 29:11

REWRITE the scripture passage in your own words. Ask your parents for help if you're not sure what it means.

HOW DOES this passage from Jeremiah encourage you? What is God saying to you here?

Hope in Action: Shae Carter's Story

Shae Carter was a 10th grader the first time she had to defend the Catholic faith. During the second week of her world religions class, her Protestant teacher began a discussion on the history of the Bible. He said ancient scholars used tests to determine which books would go in the Bible; Shae pointed out Martin Luther had removed seven books from the Bible during the 16th century.

"[I asked] how these tests proved that these other seven books did not belong in the Bible. This turned into a conversation about my Catholic faith that lasted for four months."

Shae debated her teacher after school for hours. She used writings from the Saints and early Church fathers, the Catechism, and more. But as a Protestant, "all he would listen to was Scripture."

Shae was tempted to give up hope.

Fortunately, though, Shae saw this conversation as an opportunity from our Heavenly Father. She felt confident He would not only help her find the passages she needed to counter her teacher's arguments but the kind, respectful words she needed to explain these scriptures as well. Shae's experience with her teacher led her to youth ministry: she founded the parish middle school youth group, dedicated to teaching Scriptural knowledge so members can defend their faith.

To young people who want to evangelize, Shae says not to give up hope. "Jesus chose you, knowing you weren't perfect. Not even the disciples were perfect: Peter lied about knowing Jesus; James and John asked His permission to cast fire on a city one time!"

If the disciples could go out and convert the nations, Shae says, it is possible for all of us. "You are loved, you are called, you are chosen," Shae reminds us. Dig into Scripture, she encourages, and never give up hope.

Time to Reflect

What does hope mean to you now that you've read the chapter?

WHAT STORY, scripture, quotation, or question stood out to you the most? Why? What's your greatest takeaway - the nugget of information you will carry with you?

Step by Step

Maximilian Kolbe had a posse: he relied on God and Our Lady for support. Now it's time to make your posse: your list of the people, prayers, and activities that restore hope when you feel downtrodden and alone. (Hint: turn the page)

NAME FIVE PEOPLE (saints included) who remind you of the virtues.

LIST ONE PRAYER and one scripture verse that reminds you to have hope (you can ask your parents for help on this one if you need it).

LIST ACTIVITIES and opportunities that help you practice the virtue of hope. This can include the Sacraments, daily prayer time, time with family, and so on.

7

THE SEVENTH VIRTUE: CHARITY

GROWTH MINDSET PRINCIPLE: HARD WORK AS A FORM OF
SERVICE

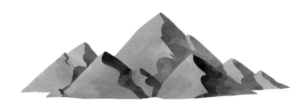

Charity is your love for God spilling out onto your neighbors. It is the love you exhibit through acts of service for the people you encounter each week.

When you practice the virtue of charity, you're preserving for the sake of others who are also children of God. You want what is best for them and work to achieve it, even when it requires difficulty.

Do you know someone who exhibits great charity? How has this person helped his fellow man?

Charity in Action:

Blessed Pier Giorgio Frassati
    Born: April 6, 1901
    Died: July 4, 1925

Pier Giorgio Frassati was a really cool guy. He climbed mountains. He loved boating and swimming. He found great peace in nature and when he had the option, he preferred to spend time outdoors.

He also had a nickname: The Terror. Turns out Frassati enjoyed playing practical jokes.

Cool factor and mischievous behavior aside, Pier Giorgio Frassati lived a life of charity. His habits and behavior gave no indication he was born to a powerful Italian family. Money was only useful to Frassati for one reason: giving it to others who needed it more.

If Frassati had money to take the train after working, he gave it to the poor and ran home instead. Frassati brought food, clothing, and necessities to the less fortunate with the St. Vincent de Paul society. Frassati also spoke out against dictators and corrupt governments, arguing publicly (and even being arrested) for Catholic social reform.

Frassati died young, a 24-year-old victim of a disease called polio. His parents expected a number of social and political dignitaries to attend their son's funeral. What they weren't prepared for, however, was the outpouring of love from the poorest in Italy. They lined the streets during his funeral procession to honor the young man who had given so much.

Frassati could have lived a life of pleasure. He was handsome, rich, and smart. But this young man's heart belonged to the cross of Christ Jesus. He loved God so much that he served his fellow humanity and never considered the cost.

Stop and Think

What impresses you the most about Pier Giorgio Frassati? How has
his example inspired you?

Just for Fun

If you could solve one problem in the world, what would it be? How
would you solve it? Write about it here.

Working for Mercy

Remember when you were little and everybody kept telling you to share? It was hard, wasn't it? Who wants to give up their favorite Ninja Turtle or the crayons they've been coloring with? Why couldn't those other kids get their own?

Truthfully, that feeling is totally normal. Up until the age of six or seven, children believe the world revolves around them alone. But you've grown up now, and sharing's taken on a different meaning. Instead of giving to people because you have to, you give to others out of love.

It's still not easy, though.

Our first instinct is self-preservation. It's not uncommon to want to hold things back, put yourself first, or keep quiet when it's time to speak up.

Fortunately, the Church in her wisdom has given us the Works of Mercy: 14 tangible ways in which we can serve our neighbor. The Works of Mercy remind us of our purpose, especially when we're doing things that are hard.

Corporal Works of Mercy (charitable acts that serve the physical person)

- Feed the hungry
- Give water to the thirsty
- Clothe the naked
- Shelter the homeless
- Visit the sick
- Visit the imprisoned
- Bury the dead

Spiritual Works of Mercy (charitable acts that serve the soul):

- Instruct the ignorant

- Counsel the doubtful
- Admonish the sinner
- Bear wrongs patiently
- Forgive offenses
- Comfort the afflicted
- Pray for the living and the dead

So yes, I know, it's still not easy to share. It's not easy to tell a friend that what he's doing won't get him into heaven, nor is it comfortable to help those who have less than you. But it matters and it's important, both for your sake and for those who need assistance. The next time you're tempted to quit, think about the long game:

What's the real purpose of what I'm doing? Who will this effort truly serve?

CONFORM OUR
LIVES TO THE TWO
COMMANDMENTS
THAT ARE THE
ESSENCE OF THE
CATHOLIC FAITH:
TO LOVE THE LORD,
OUR GOD, WITH ALL
OUR STRENGTH, AND
TO LOVE OUR
NEIGHBOR AS
OURSELVES.

-Bl. Pier Giorgio Frassati

Stop and Think

Why is it so important to love God with all your heart, and your neighbor as yourself?

∾

Let Us Pray

Heavenly Father, you blessed Pier Giorgio Frassati with a heart for charity. Help me to follow in his footsteps, loving you first and, because I love you, serving my neighbor.

AMEN

Hearing God's Voice

"Then the righteous will answer him, 'Lord, when was it that we saw you hungry and gave you food, or thirsty and gave you something to drink? And when was it that we saw you a stranger and welcomed you, or naked and gave you clothing? And when was it that we saw you sick or in prison and visited you?' And the king will answer them, 'Truly I tell you, just as you did it to one of the least of these who are members of my family, you did it to me.' MT 25:37-40

IN THIS PASSAGE, Jesus uses a parable to explain the importance of charity. Who is he referring to when he mentions "the least of these?" Ask your parents if you aren't sure.

WHY ISN'T it easy to practice charity? What tends to hold people back?

Charity in Action: Your Story

You've read the stories of four young men and women who have conquered obstacles. Use this space to write your own story or the story of someone whose charity has impressed you. How have you seen charity played out in your life or the lives of others?

Time to Reflect

What does charity mean to you now that you've read the chapter?

WHAT STORY, scripture, quotation, or question stood out to you the most? Why? What's your greatest takeaway - the nugget of information you will carry with you?

Step by Step

In the section on Working for Mercy, we talked about the big picture: specifically, seeing your efforts as the hands and feet of God.

ON THE NEXT page is a list of the Works of Mercy. Think about the challenges and difficulties you face, even the small ones that you deal with every day (for example, taking out the trash when you don't want to; doing your schoolwork or your homework; and so on). Write those challenges next to the Works of Mercy they might fall under. Don't worry if you don't have a challenge for each one.

Corporal Works of Mercy:

- Feed the hungry
- Give water to the thirsty
- Clothe the naked
- Shelter the homeless
- Visit the sick
- Visit the imprisoned
- Bury the dead

Spiritual Works of Mercy:

- Instruct the ignorant
- Counsel the doubtful
- Admonish the sinners
- Bear wrongs patiently
- Forgive offenses
- Comfort the afflicted
- Pray for the living and the dead

YOU ARE MADE FOR GREATNESS

Do not be conformed to this world, but be transformed by the renewing of your minds, so that you may discern what is the will of God—what is good and acceptable and perfect.
Romans 12:2

Throughout the course of this journal, you've begun to transform yourself for God. Like the saints, holy people, and peers who have gone before you,

- You've learned to turn your obstacles into opportunities and your stumbling blocks into stepping stones.
- You've learned about the virtues and their application to your life.
- You've discovered how each of these gifts can form and shape you into the person God has designated, even when the journey is hard.
- You've made step by step plans to develop a growth mindset rooted in Christ and his Church.

You've moved mountains, my friend, and proved you are made for greatness.

Now go out there and change this pagan world. (Adapted from a quote by Mother Angelica. Who else?)

GROWTH MINDSET REMINDERS

(FOR KIDS AND THEIR PARENTS)

Practice purposeful effort

Doing your best is commendable. Doing your best with the intent to move mountains is admirable, and more helpful in the long run.

Find joy in the process

Great minds are curious, not competitive. Embrace learning for the sake of learning and let go of the desire for awards.

Encourage reflection

Take time to evaluate the progress you have made. Ask questions like, "How have I grown?" "What have I conquered?" "What lessons have I learned that I can apply going forward?"

See weakness as an area for growth

Remember: challenges are stepping stones, not stumbling blocks. We all have weaknesses, but they neither define us nor dictate our actions.

SAY THIS, NOT THAT

(GROWTH MINDSET EDITION)

Need help building that fortress brain?

Instead of: I'm no good at this.
    Say: I'm still learning.

Instead of: I'm worthless.
    Say: I am beautifully, wonderfully made.

Instead of: There's no way I can do this. I'm scared.
    Say: I can do all things through Christ who strengthens me.

Instead of: I'm not good at this.
    Say: This is a skill I'm still working on.

Instead of: I don't even want to try.
    Say: I am made for a specific purpose. God will provide.

Instead of: I will never be that smart.
    Say: I can learn how to do this.

Instead of: I'm always making mistakes.
   Say: My mistakes help me make better decisions.

Instead of: This is way too hard.
   Say: This will take hard work, but God will help me.

Instead of: I give up.
   Say: Lord, give me the strength to persevere.

Instead of: Plan A was a bust.
   Say: Time to create a plan B!

Instead of: That's not my talent. My sister/brother/friend is better at it.
   Say: I'm proud of my sister/brother/friend. I can learn from her/him.

Instead of: I'm always messing up.
   Say: God's not finished with me yet. He will see me through.

∾

NOTES

D id something strike you as you were reading? Is there something you would like to remember, or a special note you would like to write to yourself? Use these pages to record your notes.

ABOUT THE AUTHOR

Ginny Kochis is an author, blogger, and homeschooling mom of three from Northern Virginia who believes God gives curious, creative, intense children the exact mother they need to thrive. Through her website and online community, Ginny provides practical support and prayerful encouragement to Catholic moms raising the differently-wired.

Find more resources and join 3500 moms in the Not So Formulaic community at www.notsoformulaic.com

About the Cover and Portrait Illustrator

Claire Peterson was created to create. A native Minnesotan, Claire is an accomplished watercolor artist who finds inspiration in the simple beauty of daily life. View Claire's work and connect with her at https://cpetey.wixsite.com/mysite

Made in the USA
Columbia, SC
19 November 2020